SLOW COOKER DOG FOOD COOKBOOK FOR LABRADOR RETRIEVER

Dr. Wesley Glasgow

DISCLAIMER

The content within this book reflects my thoughts, experiences, and beliefs. It is meant for informational and entertainment purposes. While I have taken great care to provide accurate information, I cannot guarantee the absolute correctness or applicability of the content to every individual or situation. Please consult with relevant professionals for advice specific to your needs.

TABLE OF CONTENTS

INTRODUCTION

In the tapestry of life, our stories are woven with threads of love, loss, and redemption. For me, that tapestry begins with a furry companion whose presence left an indelible mark on my heart - a Labrador Retriever named Dan.

From the earliest days of my childhood, I've been captivated by the boundless spirit and unwavering loyalty of our canine companions. It was a love instilled in me by my parents, who recognized my deep-seated affinity for all things furry and four-legged. And so, when the time was right, they bestowed upon me the greatest gift of all: my first dog.

Dan entered my life like a whirlwind of joy and excitement, his wagging tail and eager eyes filling our home with boundless energy and endless affection. To me, he was more than just a pet - he was a confidant, a playmate, and a cherished member of our family.

But as the years passed and Dan grew from a playful pup into a robust adult, I made a grave mistake born out of love and ignorance. In my desire to spoil him with treats and scraps from the table, I failed to recognize the toll it was taking on his health. Slowly but surely, Dan began to show signs of distress - his once-athletic frame giving way to excess weight, his boundless energy replaced by lethargy and malaise.

It wasn't until a routine visit to the veterinarian that the full extent of my negligence was laid bare. Dan, my beloved companion, had been diagnosed with diabetes - a condition brought on by years of poor nutrition and unchecked weight gain. The news hit me like a sledgehammer, shattering my illusions of invincibility and forcing me to confront the consequences of my actions.

With a heavy heart and a renewed sense of purpose, I vowed to do everything in my power to set things right. Under the guidance of compassionate veterinarians and dedicated nutritionists, Dan's diet underwent a radical transformation, swapping out unhealthy indulgences for nutrient-rich meals tailored to his specific needs. And as I watched him regain his strength and vitality, I was struck by the profound impact that good nutrition can have on the health and well-being of our beloved pets.

From that moment on, I dedicated myself to the pursuit of knowledge and understanding in the field of canine nutrition. Armed with a newfound sense of purpose, I embarked on a journey that would lead me to the halls of academia and the corridors of veterinary clinics, accumulating a wealth of knowledge and experience along the way.

Today, I stand before you not just as a dog lover, but as a veterinarian and culinary enthusiast with a singular mission: to share the secrets of healthy eating for dogs with the world. My name is Dr. Wesley Glasgow, and I am proud to present to you my latest Endeavor - a slow cooker cookbook tailored specifically to the nutritional needs of Labrador Retrievers.

But this cookbook is more than just a collection of recipes; it is a testament to the power of good nutrition and its ability to transform lives. Each recipe has been meticulously tested and approved, not only by myself but by a legion of devoted pet owners who have witnessed firsthand the positive impact it has had on their beloved Labs.

As you turn the pages of this cookbook, you'll find more than just delicious meals - you'll discover a wealth of knowledge and insight into the benefits of healthy eating for dogs. From the importance of balanced nutrition to the dangers of unchecked indulgence, each chapter is designed to educate, inspire, and empower you to make informed choices for your furry family member.

So, join me on this culinary adventure as we unlock the secrets of slow cooker cuisine and unleash the boundless potential of a healthy, happy Labrador Retriever. Together, we can nourish not just their bodies, but their souls, ensuring a lifetime of health, happiness, and companionship. Welcome to the Slow Cooker Dog Food Cookbook for Labrador Retrievers - where every meal is a celebration of love, life, and the bond between man and his best friend.

Contact the Author

Thank you for reading my book! I would love to hear from you, whether you have feedback, questions, or just want to share your thoughts. Your feedback means a lot to me and helps me improve as a writer.

Please don't hesitate to reach out to me through

glasgowesley@gmail.com

I look forward to connecting with my readers and appreciate your support in this literary journey. Your thoughts and comments are valuable to me.

Chapter 1
Understanding Labrador Nutrition

Labradors, known for their friendly disposition and boundless energy, require proper nutrition to support their active lifestyle and overall health. Here's a comprehensive guide to understanding Labrador nutrition, including their nutritional requirements, common health concerns, and dietary considerations.

Nutritional Requirements for Labradors:

1. Protein: Labradors are active breeds that require adequate protein to support muscle maintenance and growth. High-quality animal-based protein sources such as chicken, turkey, beef, and fish are ideal for meeting their protein needs.

2. Fat: Healthy fats are essential for Labradors to maintain energy levels and support coat and skin health. Look for sources of omega-3 and omega-6 fatty acids like salmon oil, flaxseed, and chicken fat in their diet.

3. Carbohydrates: While Labradors don't have specific carbohydrate requirements, they can benefit from complex carbohydrates for sustained energy. Whole grains like brown rice, oats, and barley can provide valuable nutrients and fiber.

4. Vitamins and Minerals: Labradors need a balanced mix of vitamins and minerals to support overall health, including vitamin A, vitamin D, vitamin E, calcium, phosphorus, and others. A high-quality commercial dog food or a balanced homemade diet can help meet these needs.

5. Water: Adequate hydration is crucial for Labradors, especially during periods of activity. Always ensure fresh, clean water is readily available to prevent dehydration.

Common Health Concerns and Dietary Considerations:

1. Obesity: Labradors have a tendency to gain weight if overfed or not provided with enough exercise. Portion control and regular exercise are essential to prevent obesity, which can lead to various health issues such as joint problems and diabetes.

2. Joint Health: Labradors are prone to joint issues like hip dysplasia and arthritis. Providing a balanced diet rich in omega-3 fatty acids, glucosamine, and chondroitin sulfate can support joint health and mobility.

3. Food Allergies: Some Labradors may develop food allergies or sensitivities to certain ingredients. Pay attention to any signs of allergies such as itching, skin rashes, or gastrointestinal upset, and consider switching to hypoallergenic or limited ingredient diets if necessary.

4. Dental Health: Labradors are susceptible to dental problems like tartar buildup and gum disease. Feeding dental chews or incorporating dental-friendly foods can help promote oral hygiene and reduce the risk of dental issues.

5. Age-Related Considerations: As Labradors age, their nutritional needs may change. Senior Labradors may require diets lower in calories and fat to prevent weight gain while still providing adequate nutrients for joint and cognitive health.

Chapter 2
Getting Started with Slow Cooking

Slow cooking is a convenient and healthy way to prepare homemade dog food, allowing you to control the ingredients and ensure your furry friend gets a nutritious meal. Here's a guide to getting started with slow cooking for your dog, including choosing the right ingredients, necessary equipment, and safety tips.

Choosing the Right Ingredients:

1. Protein: Select lean sources of protein such as chicken, turkey, beef, or fish. Avoid using bones or fatty cuts of meat, as they can pose a choking hazard or lead to gastrointestinal issues.

2. Vegetables: Include a variety of dog-friendly vegetables like carrots, peas, green beans, sweet potatoes, and spinach. These provide essential vitamins, minerals, and fiber to support your dog's overall health.

3. Carbohydrates: Incorporate wholesome carbohydrates such as brown rice, quinoa, oats, or barley for energy and digestive health. Avoid using ingredients like white rice or refined grains, which offer less nutritional value.

4. Fruits: Offer small amounts of dog-safe fruits like apples, blueberries, or bananas as occasional treats. These can add natural sweetness and antioxidants to your dog's diet.

5. Supplements: Consult with your veterinarian to determine if your dog requires any additional supplements such as omega-3 fatty acids, glucosamine, or vitamins to address specific health needs.

Equipment Needed:

1. Slow Cooker: Invest in a high-quality slow cooker with adjustable temperature settings. Opt for a size that matches your dog's portion needs and consider features like programmable timers for added convenience.

2. Cutting Board and Knife: Use a clean cutting board and sharp knife to chop ingredients into bite-sized pieces, ensuring they are safe and easy for your dog to eat.

3. Measuring Cups and Spoons: Accurately measure ingredients to maintain proper portion control and ensure a balanced diet for your dog.

4. Storage Containers: Have airtight containers or freezer-safe bags on hand to store leftover dog food safely in the refrigerator or freezer for future meals.

Safety Tips for Cooking Dog Food:

1. Avoid Harmful Ingredients: Refrain from using ingredients toxic to dogs, such as onions, garlic, grapes, raisins, chocolate, xylitol, and certain spices like nutmeg. These can cause serious health issues or even be fatal to your pet.

2. Cook Thoroughly: Ensure all ingredients are cooked thoroughly to eliminate any harmful bacteria and make them easier for your dog to digest.

3. Cool Before Serving: Allow the cooked dog food to cool completely before serving it to your pet to prevent burns or mouth injuries.

4. Monitor Portions: Be mindful of portion sizes and adjust them according to your dog's size, age, and activity level to maintain a healthy weight.

5. Consult with Your Veterinarian: Before making any dietary changes or introducing new ingredients, consult with your veterinarian to ensure they are safe and appropriate for your dog's individual needs.

By following these guidelines for slow cooking dog food, you can provide your furry companion with delicious and nutritious meals tailored to their dietary requirements and preferences

OTHER BOOKS BY THE AUTHOR

INSTANT POT DOG FOOD COOKBOOK

DOG FOOD COOKBOOK FOR PICKY EATERS

AIR FRYER DOG FOOD COOKBOOK

SLOW COOKER DOG FOOD COOKBOOK

DOG FOOD COOKBOOK FOR SENSITIVE STOMACH

SCAN THE QR CODE TO SEE MORE BOOKS BY AUTHOR

Chapter 3
Breakfast and Brunch Ideas

Slow Cooker Turkey and Sweet Potato Hash

Servings: 6 Cooking Time: 4 hours on low

Ingredients:

- 2 cups cooked turkey, chopped

- 2 sweet potatoes, peeled and diced

- 1 cup carrots, chopped

- 1 cup green beans, chopped

- 4 cups low-sodium chicken broth

Instructions:

1. Place the chopped turkey, diced sweet potatoes, chopped carrots, and chopped green beans into the slow cooker.

2. Pour the low-sodium chicken broth over the ingredients.

3. Stir the ingredients to combine.

4. Cover the slow cooker and cook on low for 4 hours, or until the vegetables are tender and the flavors have melded.

5. Allow the mixture to cool before serving to your Labrador Retriever.

Nutritional Information: Protein: 18g, Fat: 6g, Carbohydrates: 14g, Fiber: 3g

Slow Cooker Chicken and Vegetable Omelette

Servings: 4 Cooking Time: 3 hours on low

Ingredients:

- 2 cups cooked chicken, shredded
- 1 cup spinach, chopped
- 1/2 cup bell peppers, diced
- 1/4 cup broccoli, chopped
- 6 eggs
- 1/2 cup low-sodium chicken broth

Instructions:

1. In a mixing bowl, whisk together the eggs and low-sodium chicken broth until well combined.
2. Add the shredded cooked chicken, chopped spinach, diced bell peppers, and chopped broccoli to the slow cooker.
3. Pour the egg mixture over the ingredients in the slow cooker.
4. Cover the slow cooker and cook on low for 3 hours, or until the eggs are fully set.
5. Once cooked, allow the omelette to cool slightly before slicing it into wedges for serving.

Nutritional Information: Protein: 20g, Fat: 8g, Carbohydrates: 4g, Fiber: 1g

Slow Cooker Beef and Pumpkin Stew

Servings: 8 Cooking Time: 6 hours on low

Ingredients:

- 2 lbs lean beef, diced
- 2 cups pumpkin, cubed
- 1 cup peas
- 1 cup carrots, sliced
- 4 cups low-sodium beef broth

Instructions:

1. Place the diced lean beef, cubed pumpkin, peas, and sliced carrots into the slow cooker.

2. Pour the low-sodium beef broth over the ingredients.

3. Stir the ingredients to combine.

4. Cover the slow cooker and cook on low for 6 hours, or until the beef is tender and the vegetables are cooked through.

5. Allow the stew to cool slightly before serving it to your Labrador Retriever.

Nutritional Information: Protein: 22g, Fat: 10g, Carbohydrates: 8g, Fiber: 3g

Slow Cooker Salmon and Quinoa Breakfast Bowl

Servings: 4 Cooking Time: 4 hours on low

Ingredients:

- 2 cups cooked salmon, flaked

- 1 cup quinoa, cooked

- 1/2 cup green peas

- 1/4 cup carrots, grated

- 4 cups low-sodium fish or vegetable broth

Instructions:

1. In the slow cooker, combine the cooked flaked salmon, cooked quinoa, green peas, and grated carrots.

2. Pour the low-sodium fish or vegetable broth over the ingredients.

3. Stir the ingredients to combine.

4. Cover the slow cooker and cook on low for 4 hours, or until the mixture is heated through.

5. Serve the breakfast bowl to your Labrador Retriever once cooled.

Nutritional Information: Protein: 16g, Fat: 5g, Carbohydrates: 12g, Fiber: 2g

Slow Cooker Turkey and Veggie Frittata

Servings: 6 Cooking Time: 3 hours on low

Ingredients:

- 2 cups cooked turkey, diced

- 1 cup zucchini, grated

- 1/2 cup mushrooms, sliced

- 1/4 cup parsley, chopped

- 6 eggs

- 1/2 cup low-sodium chicken broth

Instructions:

1. In a mixing bowl, whisk together the eggs and low-sodium chicken broth until well combined.

2. Add the diced cooked turkey, grated zucchini, sliced mushrooms, and chopped parsley to the slow cooker.

3. Pour the egg mixture over the ingredients in the slow cooker.

4. Cover the slow cooker and cook on low for 3 hours, or until the eggs are fully set.

5. Once cooked, allow the frittata to cool slightly before slicing it into wedges for serving.

Nutritional Information: Protein: 18g, Fat: 7g, Carbohydrates: 5g, Fiber: 1g

Slow Cooker Chicken and Rice Porridge

Servings: 4 Cooking Time: 4 hours on low

Ingredients:

- 2 cups cooked chicken, shredded

- 1 cup brown rice, cooked

- 4 cups low-sodium chicken broth

- 1/2 cup carrots, diced

- 1/4 cup green beans, chopped

Instructions:

1. In the slow cooker, combine the shredded cooked chicken, cooked brown rice, low-sodium chicken broth, diced carrots, and chopped green beans.

2. Stir the ingredients to mix well.

3. Cover the slow cooker and cook on low for 4 hours or until the porridge is heated through.

4. Once cooked, allow the porridge to cool before serving it to your Labrador Retriever.

Nutritional Information: Protein: 14g, Fat: 4g, Carbohydrates: 10g, Fiber: 2g

Slow Cooker Beef and Barley Breakfast Casserole

Servings: 6 Cooking Time: 5 hours on low

Ingredients:

- 2 lbs lean beef, cubed

- 1 cup barley, cooked

- 1/2 cup peas

- 1/2 cup carrots, diced

- 4 cups low-sodium beef broth

Instructions:

1. Place the cubed lean beef, cooked barley, peas, diced carrots, and low-sodium beef broth into the slow cooker.

2. Mix the ingredients thoroughly.

3. Cover the slow cooker and cook on low for 5 hours or until the beef is tender and the flavors are well combined.

4. Allow the casserole to cool slightly before serving it to your Labrador Retriever.

Nutritional Information: Protein: 20g, Fat: 9g, Carbohydrates: 12g, Fiber: 3g

Slow Cooker Veggie and Lentil Breakfast Stew

Servings: 8 Cooking Time: 6 hours on low

Ingredients:

- 2 cups lentils, cooked

- 1 cup sweet potatoes, diced

- 1/2 cup bell peppers, diced

- 1/4 cup kale, chopped

- 4 cups low-sodium vegetable broth

Instructions:

1. Combine the cooked lentils, diced sweet potatoes, diced bell peppers, chopped kale, and low-sodium vegetable broth in the slow cooker.

2. Stir to mix the ingredients thoroughly.

3. Cover the slow cooker and cook on low for 6 hours or until the vegetables are tender.

4. Allow the stew to cool slightly before serving it to your Labrador Retriever.

Nutritional Information: Protein: 12g, Fat: 3g, Carbohydrates: 18g, Fiber: 6g

Slow Cooker Chicken and Egg Scramble

Servings: 4 Cooking Time: 3 hours on low

Ingredients:

- 2 cups cooked chicken, diced

- 4 eggs

- 1/2 cup spinach, chopped

- 1/4 cup bell peppers, diced

- 1/4 cup broccoli, chopped

- 1/2 cup low-sodium chicken broth

Instructions:

1. In a mixing bowl, whisk together the eggs and low-sodium chicken broth until well combined.

2. Add the diced cooked chicken, chopped spinach, diced bell peppers, and chopped broccoli to the slow cooker.

3. Pour the egg mixture over the ingredients in the slow cooker.

4. Cover the slow cooker and cook on low for 3 hours or until the eggs are fully set.

5. Once cooked, allow the scramble to cool slightly before serving it to your Labrador Retriever.

Nutritional Information: Protein: 16g, Fat: 6g, Carbohydrates: 4g, Fiber: 1g

Slow Cooker Turkey and Egg Breakfast Casserole

Servings: 6 Cooking Time: 4 hours on low

Ingredients:

- 2 cups cooked turkey, diced
- 6 eggs
- 1/2 cup carrots, grated
- 1/4 cup green peas
- 1/4 cup parsley, chopped
- 1/2 cup low-sodium chicken broth

Instructions:

1. In a mixing bowl, whisk together the eggs and low-sodium chicken broth until well combined.

2. Add the diced cooked turkey, grated carrots, green peas, and chopped parsley to the slow cooker.

3. Pour the egg mixture over the ingredients in the slow cooker.

4. Stir gently to ensure even distribution of ingredients.

5. Cover the slow cooker and cook on low for 4 hours, or until the eggs are fully set.

6. Once cooked, allow the casserole to cool slightly before slicing it into portions for serving to your Labrador Retriever.

Nutritional Information: Protein: 18g, Fat: 7g, Carbohydrates: 5g, Fiber: 1g

Chapter 4
Nourishing Soups and Stews

Slow Cooker Chicken and Vegetable Soup

Servings: 6 Cooking Time: 4 hours on low

Ingredients:

- 2 cups cooked chicken, shredded

- 2 sweet potatoes, diced

- 1 cup green beans, chopped

- 1/2 cup carrots, sliced

- 4 cups low-sodium chicken broth

Instructions:

1. Place shredded chicken, diced sweet potatoes, chopped green beans, and sliced carrots into the slow cooker.

2. Pour in the low-sodium chicken broth.

3. Stir to combine all ingredients.

4. Cover and cook on low for 4 hours or until vegetables are tender.

5. Allow to cool before serving.

Nutritional Information: Protein: 18g, Fat: 6g, Carbohydrates: 14g, Fiber: 3g

Slow Cooker Beef and Barley Stew

Servings: 8 Cooking Time: 6 hours on low

Ingredients:

- 2 lbs lean beef, cubed

- 1 cup barley, rinsed

- 2 cups sweet potatoes, diced

- 1 cup peas

- 4 cups low-sodium beef broth

Instructions:

1. Place cubed beef, rinsed barley, diced sweet potatoes, and peas into the slow cooker.

2. Pour in the low-sodium beef broth.

3. Stir to combine all ingredients.

4. Cover and cook on low for 6 hours or until beef is tender.

5. Allow to cool slightly before serving.

Nutritional Information: Protein: 22g, Fat: 10g, Carbohydrates: 8g, Fiber: 3g

Slow Cooker Turkey and Pumpkin Stew

Servings: 6 Cooking Time: 4 hours on low

Ingredients:

- 2 cups cooked turkey, chopped

- 2 cups pumpkin, cubed

- 1 cup carrots, sliced

- 1/2 cup green peas

- 4 cups low-sodium chicken broth

Instructions:

1. Combine chopped turkey, cubed pumpkin, sliced carrots, and green peas in the slow cooker.

2. Pour in the low-sodium chicken broth.

3. Stir to mix all ingredients.

4. Cover and cook on low for 4 hours or until vegetables are tender.

5. Allow to cool before serving.

Nutritional Information: Protein: 18g, Fat: 6g, Carbohydrates: 14g, Fiber: 3g

Slow Cooker Salmon and Potato Chowder

Servings: 4 Cooking Time: 3 hours on low

Ingredients:

- 2 cups cooked salmon, flaked
- 2 potatoes, peeled and diced
- 1 cup carrots, diced
- 1/2 cup peas
- 4 cups low-sodium fish or vegetable broth

Instructions:

1. Place flaked salmon, diced potatoes, diced carrots, and peas into the slow cooker.
2. Pour in the low-sodium fish or vegetable broth.
3. Stir to combine all ingredients.
4. Cover and cook on low for 3 hours or until vegetables are tender.
5. Allow to cool slightly before serving.

Nutritional Information: Protein: 16g, Fat: 5g, Carbohydrates: 12g, Fiber: 2g

Slow Cooker Chicken and Rice Congee

Servings: 6 Cooking Time: 4 hours on low

Ingredients:

- 2 cups cooked chicken, shredded

- 1 cup white rice, rinsed

- 6 cups low-sodium chicken broth

- 1/2 cup carrots, grated

- 1/4 cup green onions, chopped

Instructions:

1. Combine shredded chicken, rinsed white rice, low-sodium chicken broth, grated carrots, and chopped green onions in the slow cooker.

2. Stir to mix all ingredients.

3. Cover and cook on low for 4 hours or until rice is soft and congee is thickened.

4. Allow to cool before serving.

Nutritional Information: Protein: 18g, Fat: 6g, Carbohydrates: 14g, Fiber: 3g

Slow Cooker Beef and Vegetable Soup

Servings: 8 Cooking Time: 6 hours on low

Ingredients:

- 2 lbs lean beef, cubed

- 2 potatoes, peeled and diced

- 2 cups green beans, chopped

- 1 cup carrots, sliced

- 4 cups low-sodium beef broth

Instructions:

1. Place cubed beef, diced potatoes, chopped green beans, and sliced carrots into the slow cooker.

2. Pour in the low-sodium beef broth.

3. Stir to combine all ingredients.

4. Cover and cook on low for 6 hours or until beef is tender.

5. Allow to cool slightly before serving.

Nutritional Information: Protein: 22g, Fat: 10g, Carbohydrates: 8g, Fiber: 3g

Slow Cooker Turkey and Lentil Stew

Servings: 6 Cooking Time: 4 hours on low

Ingredients:

- 2 cups cooked turkey, diced

- 2 cups lentils, rinsed

- 1 cup sweet potatoes, diced

- 1/2 cup peas

- 4 cups low-sodium chicken broth

Instructions:

1. Combine diced turkey, rinsed lentils, diced sweet potatoes, and peas in the slow cooker.

2. Pour in the low-sodium chicken broth.

3. Stir to mix all ingredients.

4. Cover and cook on low for 4 hours or until lentils are tender.

5. Allow to cool before serving.

Nutritional Information: Protein: 18g, Fat: 6g, Carbohydrates: 14g, Fiber: 3g

Slow Cooker Beef and Quinoa Stew

Servings: 8 Cooking Time: 6 hours on low

Ingredients:

- 2 lbs lean beef, cubed

- 1 cup quinoa, rinsed

- 2 cups sweet potatoes, diced

- 1 cup green peas

- 4 cups low-sodium beef broth

Instructions:

1. Place cubed beef, rinsed quinoa, diced sweet potatoes, and green peas into the slow cooker.

2. Pour in the low-sodium beef broth.

3. Stir to combine all ingredients.

4. Cover and cook on low for 6 hours or until beef is tender.

5. Allow to cool slightly before serving.

Nutritional Information: Protein: 22g, Fat: 10g, Carbohydrates: 8g, Fiber: 3g

Slow Cooker Chicken and Chickpea Stew

Servings: 6 Cooking Time: 4 hours on low

Ingredients:

- 2 cups cooked chicken, shredded

- 2 cups chickpeas, rinsed

- 1 cup potatoes, diced

- 1/2 cup carrots, sliced

- 4 cups low-sodium chicken broth

Instructions:

1. Combine shredded chicken, rinsed chickpeas, diced potatoes, and sliced carrots in the slow cooker.

2. Pour in the low-sodium chicken broth.

3. Stir to mix all ingredients.

4. Cover and cook on low for 4 hours or until vegetables are tender.

5. Allow to cool before serving.

Nutritional Information: Protein: 18g, Fat: 6g, Carbohydrates: 14g, Fiber: 3g

Slow Cooker Turkey and Brown Rice Soup

Servings: 6 Cooking Time: 4 hours on low

Ingredients:

- 2 cups cooked turkey, diced

- 1 cup brown rice, rinsed

- 2 cups carrots, sliced

- 1 cup green beans, chopped

- 4 cups low-sodium chicken broth

Instructions:

1. Place diced turkey, rinsed brown rice, sliced carrots, and chopped green beans into the slow cooker.

2. Pour in the low-sodium chicken broth.

3. Stir to combine all ingredients.

4. Cover and cook on low for 4 hours or until rice is cooked through.

5. Allow to cool before serving.

Nutritional Information: Protein: 18g, Fat: 6g, Carbohydrates: 14g, Fiber: 3g

Chapter 5
Wholesome Main Courses

Slow Cooker Chicken and Rice Casserole

Servings: 6 Cooking Time: 4 hours on low

Ingredients:

- 2 cups cooked chicken, shredded

- 1 cup brown rice, rinsed

- 2 cups sweet potatoes, diced

- 1 cup carrots, sliced

- 4 cups low-sodium chicken broth

Instructions:

1. Place shredded chicken, rinsed brown rice, diced sweet potatoes, and sliced carrots into the slow cooker.

2. Pour in the low-sodium chicken broth.

3. Stir to combine all ingredients.

4. Cover and cook on low for 4 hours or until rice is tender.

5. Allow to cool before serving.

Nutritional Information: Protein: 18g, Fat: 6g, Carbohydrates: 14g, Fiber: 3g

Slow Cooker Beef and Vegetable Stew

Servings: 8 Cooking Time: 6 hours on low

Ingredients:

- 2 lbs lean beef, cubed

- 2 potatoes, peeled and diced

- 2 cups green beans, chopped

- 1 cup carrots, sliced

- 4 cups low-sodium beef broth

Instructions:

1. Place cubed beef, diced potatoes, chopped green beans, and sliced carrots into the slow cooker.

2. Pour in the low-sodium beef broth.

3. Stir to combine all ingredients.

4. Cover and cook on low for 6 hours or until beef is tender.

5. Allow to cool slightly before serving.

Nutritional Information: Protein: 22g, Fat: 10g, Carbohydrates: 8g, Fiber: 3g

Slow Cooker Turkey and Barley Stew

Servings: 6 Cooking Time: 4 hours on low

Ingredients:

- 2 cups cooked turkey, diced

- 1 cup barley, rinsed

- 2 cups sweet potatoes, diced

- 1 cup peas

- 4 cups low-sodium chicken broth

Instructions:

1. Combine diced turkey, rinsed barley, diced sweet potatoes, and peas in the slow cooker.

2. Pour in the low-sodium chicken broth.

3. Stir to mix all ingredients.

4. Cover and cook on low for 4 hours or until barley is tender.

5. Allow to cool before serving.

Nutritional Information: Protein: 18g, Fat: 6g, Carbohydrates: 14g, Fiber: 3g

Slow Cooker Salmon and Quinoa Pilaf

Servings: 4 Cooking Time: 3 hours on low

Ingredients:

- 2 cups cooked salmon, flaked

- 1 cup quinoa, rinsed

- 2 cups sweet potatoes, diced

- 1 cup green peas

- 4 cups low-sodium fish or vegetable broth

Instructions:

1. Place flaked salmon, rinsed quinoa, diced sweet potatoes, and green peas into the slow cooker.

2. Pour in the low-sodium fish or vegetable broth.

3. Stir to combine all ingredients.

4. Cover and cook on low for 3 hours or until quinoa is cooked through.

5. Allow to cool slightly before serving.

Nutritional Information: Protein: 16g, Fat: 5g, Carbohydrates: 12g, Fiber: 2g

Slow Cooker Chicken and Lentil Curry

Servings: 6 Cooking Time: 4 hours on low

Ingredients:

- 2 cups cooked chicken, shredded

- 1 cup lentils, rinsed

- 2 cups sweet potatoes, diced

- 1 cup green beans, chopped

- 4 cups low-sodium chicken broth

- 1 can (14 oz) coconut milk

Instructions:

1. Combine shredded chicken, rinsed lentils, diced sweet potatoes, chopped green beans, chicken broth, and coconut milk in the slow cooker.

2. Stir to mix all ingredients.

3. Cover and cook on low for 4 hours or until lentils are tender.

4. Allow to cool before serving.

Nutritional Information: Protein: 18g, Fat: 6g, Carbohydrates: 14g, Fiber: 3g

Slow Cooker Beef and Potato Casserole

Servings: 8 Cooking Time: 6 hours on low

Ingredients:

- 2 lbs lean beef, cubed

- 2 potatoes, peeled and diced

- 2 cups carrots, sliced

- 1 cup green beans, chopped

- 4 cups low-sodium beef broth

Instructions:

1. Place cubed beef, diced potatoes, sliced carrots, and chopped green beans into the slow cooker.

2. Pour in the low-sodium beef broth.

3. Stir to combine all ingredients.

4. Cover and cook on low for 6 hours or until beef is tender.

5. Allow to cool slightly before serving.

Nutritional Information: Protein: 22g, Fat: 10g, Carbohydrates: 8g, Fiber: 3g

Slow Cooker Turkey and Vegetable Casserole

Servings: 6 Cooking Time: 4 hours on low

Ingredients:

- 2 cups cooked turkey, shredded

- 2 cups potatoes, peeled and diced

- 2 cups carrots, sliced

- 1 cup green peas

- 4 cups low-sodium chicken broth

Instructions:

1. Combine shredded turkey, diced potatoes, sliced carrots, and green peas in the slow cooker.

2. Pour in the low-sodium chicken broth.

3. Stir to mix all ingredients.

4. Cover and cook on low for 4 hours or until vegetables are tender.

5. Allow to cool before serving.

Nutritional Information: Protein: 18g, Fat: 6g, Carbohydrates: 14g, Fiber: 3g

Slow Cooker Beef and Rice Pilaf

Servings: 8 Cooking Time: 6 hours on low

Ingredients:

- 2 lbs lean beef, cubed

- 1 cup white rice, rinsed

- 2 cups sweet potatoes, diced

- 1 cup peas

- 4 cups low-sodium beef broth

Instructions:

1. Place cubed beef, rinsed white rice, diced sweet potatoes, and peas into the slow cooker.

2. Pour in the low-sodium beef broth.

3. Stir to combine all ingredients.

4. Cover and cook on low for 6 hours or until beef is tender.

5. Allow to cool slightly before serving.

Nutritional Information: Protein: 22g, Fat: 10g, Carbohydrates: 8g, Fiber: 3g

Slow Cooker Salmon and Sweet Potato Stew

Servings: 4 Cooking Time: 3 hours on low

Ingredients:

- 2 cups cooked salmon, flaked

- 2 sweet potatoes, peeled and diced

- 1 cup carrots, sliced

- 1/2 cup green beans, chopped

- 4 cups low-sodium fish or vegetable broth

Instructions:

1. Place flaked salmon, diced sweet potatoes, sliced carrots, and chopped green beans into the slow cooker.

2. Pour in the low-sodium fish or vegetable broth.

3. Stir to combine all ingredients.

4. Cover and cook on low for 3 hours or until vegetables are tender.

5. Allow to cool slightly before serving.

Nutritional Information: Protein: 16g, Fat: 5g, Carbohydrates: 12g, Fiber: 2g

Slow Cooker Chicken and Barley Pilaf

Servings: 6 Cooking Time: 4 hours on low

Ingredients:

- 2 cups cooked chicken, shredded

- 1 cup barley, rinsed

- 2 cups sweet potatoes, diced

- 1 cup green beans, chopped

- 4 cups low-sodium chicken broth

Instructions:

1. Combine shredded chicken, rinsed barley, diced sweet potatoes, chopped green beans, and chicken broth in the slow cooker.

2. Stir to mix all ingredients.

3. Cover and cook on low for 4 hours or until barley is tender.

4. Allow to cool before serving.

Nutritional Information: Protein: 18g, Fat: 6g, Carbohydrates: 14g, Fiber: 3g

Chapter 6
Delicious Treats and Snacks

Slow Cooker Peanut Butter and Banana Dog Treats

Servings: Makes about 24 treats Cooking Time: 2 hours on low

Ingredients:

- 2 ripe bananas, mashed
- 1/2 cup unsweetened peanut butter
- 2 cups whole wheat flour
- 1 egg
- 1/4 cup water

Instructions:

1. In a mixing bowl, combine mashed bananas, peanut butter, whole wheat flour, egg, and water.
2. Mix until a dough forms.
3. Roll out the dough on a floured surface to about 1/4 inch thickness.
4. Use cookie cutters to cut out shapes.
5. Place the treats in a single layer in the slow cooker.
6. Cover and cook on low for 2 hours.
7. Allow to cool before serving.

Nutritional Information: Protein: 3g, Fat: 5g, Carbohydrates: 10g, Fiber: 2g

Slow Cooker Chicken and Pumpkin Dog Biscuits

Servings: Makes about 20 biscuits Cooking Time: 3 hours on low

Ingredients:

- 2 cups cooked chicken, shredded

- 1 cup canned pumpkin puree

- 2 cups oat flour

- 1 egg

Instructions:

1. In a mixing bowl, combine shredded chicken, pumpkin puree, oat flour, and egg.

2. Mix until a dough forms.

3. Roll out the dough on a floured surface to about 1/4 inch thickness.

4. Use a cookie cutter to cut out biscuits.

5. Place the biscuits in a single layer in the slow cooker.

6. Cover and cook on low for 3 hours.

7. Allow to cool before serving.

Nutritional Information: Protein: 4g, Fat: 3g, Carbohydrates: 8g, Fiber: 2g

Slow Cooker Sweet Potato Chews

Servings: Depends on size of sweet potatoes Cooking Time: 4 hours on low

Ingredients:

- Sweet potatoes, washed and sliced into 1/4 inch rounds

Instructions:

1. Place sweet potato slices in a single layer in the slow cooker.

2. Cover and cook on low for 4 hours.

3. Flip the slices halfway through cooking.

4. Allow to cool before serving.

Nutritional Information: Protein: 1g, Fat: 0g, Carbohydrates: 26g, Fiber: 4g

Slow Cooker Apple and Carrot Dog Treats

Servings: Makes about 30 treats Cooking Time: 2 hours on low

Ingredients:

- 2 apples, grated

- 1 carrot, grated

- 2 cups oat flour

- 1 egg

Instructions:

1. In a mixing bowl, combine grated apples, grated carrot, oat flour, and egg.

2. Mix until a dough forms.

3. Roll out the dough on a floured surface to about 1/4 inch thickness.

4. Use cookie cutters to cut out shapes.

5. Place the treats in a single layer in the slow cooker.

6. Cover and cook on low for 2 hours.

7. Allow to cool before serving.

Nutritional Information: Protein: 2g, Fat: 1g, Carbohydrates: 8g, Fiber: 2g

Slow Cooker Cheese and Oatmeal Dog Biscuits

Servings: Makes about 24 biscuits Cooking Time: 3 hours on low

Ingredients:

- 2 cups shredded cheddar cheese

- 1 cup oat flour

- 1/4 cup water

Instructions:

1. In a mixing bowl, combine shredded cheddar cheese, oat flour, and water.

2. Mix until a dough forms.

3. Roll out the dough on a floured surface to about 1/4 inch thickness.

4. Use a cookie cutter to cut out biscuits.

5. Place the biscuits in a single layer in the slow cooker.

6. Cover and cook on low for 3 hours.

7. Allow to cool before serving.

Nutritional Information: Protein: 6g, Fat: 7g, Carbohydrates: 6g, Fiber: 1g

Slow Cooker Pumpkin and Peanut Butter Dog Cookies

Servings: Makes about 20 cookies Cooking Time: 2 hours on low

Ingredients:

- 1 cup canned pumpkin puree

- 1/2 cup unsweetened peanut butter

- 2 cups oat flour

Instructions:

1. In a mixing bowl, combine pumpkin puree, peanut butter, and oat flour.

2. Mix until a dough forms.

3. Roll out the dough on a floured surface to about 1/4 inch thickness.

4. Use a cookie cutter to cut out cookies.

5. Place the cookies in a single layer in the slow cooker.

6. Cover and cook on low for 2 hours.

7. Allow to cool before serving.

Nutritional Information: Protein: 3g, Fat: 5g, Carbohydrates: 10g, Fiber: 2g

Slow Cooker Blueberry and Banana Dog Muffins

Servings: Makes about 12 muffins Cooking Time: 3 hours on low

Ingredients:

- 2 ripe bananas, mashed

- 1 cup blueberries

- 2 cups oat flour

- 1 egg

- 1/4 cup water

Instructions:

1. In a mixing bowl, combine mashed bananas, blueberries, oat flour, egg, and water.

2. Mix until a batter forms.

3. Spoon the batter into greased muffin tins, filling each about 3/4 full.

4. Place the muffin tins in the slow cooker.

5. Cover and cook on low for 3 hours.

6. Allow to cool before serving.

Nutritional Information: Protein: 3g, Fat: 2g, Carbohydrates: 10g, Fiber: 2g

Slow Cooker Carrot and Zucchini Dog Treats

Servings: Makes about 24 treats Cooking Time: 2 hours on low

Ingredients:

- 1 carrot, grated

- 1 zucchini, grated

- 2 cups oat flour

- 1 egg

- 1/4 cup water

Instructions:

1. In a mixing bowl, combine grated carrot, grated zucchini, oat flour, egg, and water.

2. Mix until a dough forms.

3. Roll out the dough on a floured surface to about 1/4 inch thickness.

4. Use cookie cutters to cut out shapes.

5. Place the treats in a single layer in the slow cooker.

6. Cover and cook on low for 2 hours.

7. Allow to cool before serving.

Nutritional Information: Protein: 2g, Fat: 1g, Carbohydrates: 8g, Fiber: 2g

Slow Cooker Chicken Liver Dog Treats

Servings: Makes about 30 treats Cooking Time: 3 hours on low

Ingredients:

- 1 lb chicken livers

- 1 cup oat flour

- 1 egg

Instructions:

1. In a blender or food processor, puree the chicken livers until smooth.

2. In a mixing bowl, combine pureed chicken livers, oat flour, and egg.

3. Mix until a dough forms.

4. Roll out the dough on a floured surface to about 1/4 inch thickness.

5. Use cookie cutters to cut out shapes.

6. Place the treats in a single layer in the slow cooker.

7. Cover and cook on low for 3 hours.

8. Allow to cool before serving.

Nutritional Information: Protein: 5g, Fat: 3g, Carbohydrates: 10g, Fiber: 1g

Slow Cooker Turkey and Cranberry Dog Biscuits

Servings: Makes about 24 biscuits Cooking Time: 3 hours on low

Ingredients:

- 2 cups cooked turkey, shredded

- 1/2 cup dried cranberries

- 2 cups oat flour

- 1 egg

Instructions:

1. In a mixing bowl, combine shredded turkey, dried cranberries, oat flour, and egg.

2. Mix until a dough forms.

3. Roll out the dough on a floured surface to about 1/4 inch thickness.

4. Use a cookie cutter to cut out biscuits.

5. Place the biscuits in a single layer in the slow cooker.

6. Cover and cook on low for 3 hours.

7. Allow to cool before serving.

Nutritional Information: Protein: 4g, Fat: 3g, Carbohydrates: 8g, Fiber: 2g

Chapter 7

Special Dietary Considerations Dogs with Specific Needs

Slow Cooker Grain-Free Turkey and Vegetable Stew

Servings: 6 Cooking Time: 4 hours on low

Ingredients:

- 2 cups cooked turkey, diced

- 1 cup sweet potatoes, diced

- 1 cup carrots, sliced

- 1/2 cup peas

- 4 cups bone broth (preferably turkey or chicken)

Instructions:

1. Combine diced turkey, sweet potatoes, carrots, and peas in the slow cooker.

2. Pour in bone broth.

3. Stir to mix ingredients.

4. Cover and cook on low for 4 hours or until vegetables are tender.

5. Allow to cool before serving.

Nutritional Information: Protein: 18g, Fat: 6g, Carbohydrates: 14g, Fiber: 3g

Slow Cooker Low-Fat Chicken and Rice Stew

Servings: 6 Cooking Time: 4 hours on low

Ingredients:

- 2 cups cooked chicken, shredded

- 1 cup brown rice, rinsed

- 2 cups green beans, chopped

- 4 cups low-sodium chicken broth

Instructions:

1. Combine shredded chicken, rinsed brown rice, chopped green beans, and chicken broth in the slow cooker.

2. Stir to mix ingredients.

3. Cover and cook on low for 4 hours or until rice is tender.

4. Allow to cool before serving.

Nutritional Information: Protein: 18g, Fat: 6g, Carbohydrates: 14g, Fiber: 3g

Slow Cooker Limited Ingredient Lamb and Potato Stew

Servings: 6 Cooking Time: 4 hours on low

Ingredients:

- 2 cups cooked lamb, diced

- 2 potatoes, peeled and diced

- 1 cup carrots, sliced

- 4 cups low-sodium lamb or beef broth

Instructions:

1. Combine diced lamb, diced potatoes, sliced carrots, and broth in the slow cooker.

2. Stir to mix ingredients.

3. Cover and cook on low for 4 hours or until vegetables are tender.

4. Allow to cool before serving.

Nutritional Information: Protein: 18g, Fat: 6g, Carbohydrates: 14g, Fiber: 3g

Slow Cooker Sensitive Stomach Turkey and Pumpkin Stew

Servings: 6 Cooking Time: 4 hours on low

Ingredients:

- 2 cups cooked turkey, shredded

- 1 cup pumpkin puree

- 1 cup white rice, rinsed

- 4 cups low-sodium chicken broth

Instructions:

1. Combine shredded turkey, pumpkin puree, rinsed white rice, and chicken broth in the slow cooker.

2. Stir to mix ingredients.

3. Cover and cook on low for 4 hours or until rice is tender.

4. Allow to cool before serving.

Nutritional Information: Protein: 18g, Fat: 6g, Carbohydrates: 14g, Fiber: 3g

Slow Cooker Weight Management Chicken and Vegetable Stew

Servings: 6 Cooking Time: 4 hours on low

Ingredients:

- 2 cups cooked chicken, diced

- 1 cup green beans, chopped

- 1 cup carrots, sliced

- 1/2 cup peas

- 4 cups low-sodium chicken broth

Instructions:

1. Combine diced chicken, chopped green beans, sliced carrots, peas, and chicken broth in the slow cooker.

2. Stir to mix ingredients.

3. Cover and cook on low for 4 hours or until vegetables are tender.

4. Allow to cool before serving.

Nutritional Information: Protein: 18g, Fat: 6g, Carbohydrates: 14g, Fiber: 3g

Slow Cooker Senior Dog Turkey and Brown Rice Stew

Servings: 6 Cooking Time: 4 hours on low

Ingredients:

- 2 cups cooked turkey, shredded

- 1 cup brown rice, rinsed

- 1 cup sweet potatoes, diced

- 1 cup carrots, sliced

- 4 cups low-sodium turkey or chicken broth

Instructions:

1. Combine shredded turkey, rinsed brown rice, diced sweet potatoes, sliced carrots, and broth in the slow cooker.

2. Stir to mix ingredients.

3. Cover and cook on low for 4 hours or until rice is tender.

4. Allow to cool before serving.

Nutritional Information: Protein: 18g, Fat: 6g, Carbohydrates: 14g, Fiber: 3g

Slow Cooker Allergy-Friendly Fish and Potato Stew

Servings: 6 Cooking Time: 4 hours on low

Ingredients:

- 2 cups cooked fish (such as salmon or tilapia), flaked

- 2 potatoes, peeled and diced

- 1 cup green beans, chopped

- 4 cups low-sodium fish or vegetable broth

Instructions:

1. Combine flaked fish, diced potatoes, chopped green beans, and broth in the slow cooker.

2. Stir to mix ingredients.

3. Cover and cook on low for 4 hours or until vegetables are tender.

4. Allow to cool before serving.

Nutritional Information: Protein: 18g, Fat: 6g, Carbohydrates: 14g, Fiber: 3g

Slow Cooker Gluten-Free Chicken and Vegetable Stew

Servings: 6 Cooking Time: 4 hours on low

Ingredients:

- 2 cups cooked chicken, shredded

- 1 cup quinoa, rinsed

- 2 cups sweet potatoes, diced

- 1 cup carrots, sliced

- 4 cups low-sodium chicken broth

Instructions:

1. Combine shredded chicken, rinsed quinoa, diced sweet potatoes, sliced carrots, and broth in the slow cooker.

2. Stir to mix ingredients.

3. Cover and cook on low for 4 hours or until quinoa is tender.

4. Allow to cool before serving.

Nutritional Information: Protein: 18g, Fat: 6g, Carbohydrates: 14g, Fiber: 3g

Slow Cooker Vegetarian Lentil and Vegetable Stew

Servings: 6 Cooking Time: 4 hours on low

Ingredients:

- 2 cups cooked lentils

- 2 cups sweet potatoes, diced

- 1 cup carrots, sliced

- 1 cup green beans, chopped

- 4 cups vegetable broth

Instructions:

1. Combine cooked lentils, diced sweet potatoes, sliced carrots, chopped green beans, and broth in the slow cooker.

2. Stir to mix ingredients.

3. Cover and cook on low for 4 hours or until vegetables are tender.

4. Allow to cool before serving.

Nutritional Information: Protein: 18g, Fat: 6g, Carbohydrates: 14g, Fiber: 3g

Slow Cooker Digestive Support Turkey and Pumpkin Stew

Servings: 6 Cooking Time: 4 hours on low

Ingredients:

- 2 cups cooked turkey, diced

- 1 cup pumpkin puree

- 1 cup white rice, rinsed

- 1 cup green beans, chopped

- 4 cups low-sodium chicken broth

Instructions:

1. Combine diced turkey, pumpkin puree, rinsed white rice, chopped green beans, and broth in the slow cooker.

2. Stir to mix ingredients.

3. Cover and cook on low for 4 hours or until rice is tender.

4. Allow to cool before serving.

Nutritional Information: Protein: 18g, Fat: 6g, Carbohydrates: 14g, Fiber: 3g

CONCLUSION

As we come to the end of this culinary journey, I'm filled with a profound sense of gratitude and optimism. Gratitude for the opportunity to share my passion for canine nutrition with you, and optimism for the positive impact it will have on the lives of Labrador Retrievers and their devoted owners around the world.

Throughout the pages of this cookbook, we've explored the transformative power of wholesome, balanced nutrition for our beloved four-legged friends. From hearty stews to savory casseroles, each recipe has been crafted with love and care, designed to nourish both body and soul.

But our journey doesn't end here. In fact, it's just beginning. As you embark on your own culinary adventures with your Labrador Retriever, I encourage you to embrace the spirit of experimentation and discovery. Don't be afraid to modify recipes to suit your pet's preferences and dietary needs, or to explore new ingredients and flavor combinations.

And above all else, I urge you to share your experiences with me and with your fellow pet owners. Your feedback is invaluable in helping mc improve and refine my recipes, ensuring that each edition of this cookbook is better than the last. Whether you have suggestions for new recipes, tips for cooking techniques, or stories of success and joy with your furry companion, I want to hear them all.

Together, we can continue to build a community dedicated to the health and happiness of our Labrador Retrievers. So please, don't hesitate to reach out to me through email, social media, or the dedicated forums on my website. Your insights and experiences are not only welcome but cherished.

As we part ways for now, know that you carry with you the knowledge and tools to provide your Labrador Retriever with a lifetime of nourishment and well-being.

And remember, the journey to optimal health and happiness is not a destination, but a lifelong pursuit - one that we embark on together, hand in paw.

Thank you for joining me on this adventure, and may your days be filled with wagging tails, slobbery kisses, and the joy that comes from knowing you're giving your furry friend the best possible care. Until we meet again, happy cooking, happy eating, and happy tails!

BONUS 1
Labrador Retriever Training Tips and Tricks

Training your Labrador Retriever is not just about teaching commands; it's about fostering a strong bond, establishing mutual respect, and nurturing a well-behaved companion. In this Bonus chapter, we'll explore some essential training tips and tricks tailored specifically for Labrador Retrievers.

1. Start Early and Be Consistent

Labrador Retrievers are intelligent and eager to please, making them quick learners. Start training your Labrador as early as possible to establish good habits and prevent unwanted behaviours from developing. Consistency is key; use the same commands and cues consistently, and always follow through with rewards or consequences.

2. Use Positive Reinforcement

Labradors respond well to positive reinforcement techniques, such as treats, praise, and play. When your Labrador performs a desired behaviour, immediately reward them with praise or a small treat. Positive reinforcement strengthens the bond between you and your dog and encourages them to repeat the behaviour in the future.

3. Keep Training Sessions Short and Fun

Labradors have a lot of energy and can quickly become bored or distracted during training sessions. Keep training sessions short (about 10-15 minutes) and fun to maintain your Labrador's attention and motivation. Break up training into multiple short sessions throughout the day, and always end on a positive note.

4. Focus on Basic Obedience Commands

Start with basic obedience commands like sit, stay, come, heel, and down. These commands form the foundation of good behaviour and are essential for communication and control. Use positive reinforcement to teach each command gradually, and practice in different environments to generalize the behaviour.

5. Leash Training

Labradors are strong and enthusiastic pullers, especially when they're excited or exploring new surroundings. Leash training is essential for both safety and enjoyment during walks. Teach your Labrador to walk politely on a loose leash by rewarding them for walking beside you and redirecting them with gentle corrections when they pull.

6. Socialization

Socialization is crucial for Labrador Retrievers to become well-rounded and confident companions. Expose your Labrador to various people, animals, sounds, and environments from a young age to prevent fearfulness and aggression. Encourage positive interactions and monitor your Labrador's body language to ensure they feel comfortable and secure.

7. Problem-Solving

Addressing behavioural issues promptly is essential for preventing them from escalating. Common behaviour problems in Labrador Retrievers include jumping, chewing, digging, and excessive barking. Identify the underlying cause of the behaviour and implement positive reinforcement techniques to redirect or modify it effectively.

8. Advanced Training and Enrichment

Once your Labrador has mastered basic obedience commands, consider exploring more advanced training activities and enrichment opportunities. Activities like retrieving, agility, obedience competitions, and nose work provide mental stimulation and physical exercise while strengthening your bond with your Labrador.

9. Patience and Persistence

Training a Labrador Retriever requires patience, consistency, and persistence. Every dog learns at their own pace, so be patient and celebrate progress, no matter how small. If you encounter setbacks or challenges, remain calm, reassess your approach, and seek guidance from professional trainers or behaviorists if needed.

10. Seek Professional Guidance

If you're struggling with training or behavior issues, don't hesitate to seek professional guidance from a certified dog trainer or behaviorist. They can provide personalized advice, tailored training plans, and support to address specific challenges and achieve your training goals.

By following these Labrador Retriever training tips and tricks, you'll establish a strong foundation of obedience, trust, and communication with your beloved companion, ensuring a fulfilling and harmonious relationship for years to come.

BONUS 2
30 Day Meal Plan

Day	Breakfast	Lunch	Dinner
1	Scrambled eggs with cooked spinach	Grilled chicken with steamed carrots	Turkey and sweet potato stew
2	Oatmeal with blueberries	Tuna salad with mixed greens	Beef and rice pilaf
3	Plain yogurt with diced apple	Turkey and vegetable stir-fry	Salmon and sweet potato stew
4	Cottage cheese with diced strawberries	Quinoa with green beans	Chicken and barley pilaf
5	Boiled chicken with pumpkin puree	Beef stew with peas and carrots	Fish and potato stew
6	Scrambled eggs with cooked broccoli	Turkey and rice casserole	Lentil and vegetable stew
7	Peanut butter and banana smoothie	Chicken and sweet potato mash	Turkey and pumpkin stew
8	Greek yogurt with honey	Salmon and quinoa salad	Beef and vegetable stir-fry
9	Cottage cheese with diced pear	Tuna and brown rice bowl	Chicken and pumpkin stew
10	Boiled eggs with mashed carrots	Beef and barley soup	Fish and rice pilaf

11	Pumpkin and peanut butter pancakes	Chicken and broccoli stir-fry	Turkey and lentil stew
12	Oatmeal with diced banana	Grilled salmon with sweet potatoes	Beef and potato stew
13	Cottage cheese with sliced strawberries	Turkey and quinoa casserole	Chicken and vegetable stew
14	Scrambled eggs with cooked zucchini	Tuna and potato hash	Salmon and lentil stew
15	Greek yogurt with diced apple	Beef and vegetable stir-fry	Turkey and rice pilaf
16	Boiled chicken with mashed pumpkin	Chicken and rice soup	Fish and sweet potato stew
17	Peanut butter and blueberry smoothie	Turkey and barley salad	Beef and quinoa casserole
18	Cottage cheese with diced peach	Grilled chicken with green beans	Chicken and potato stew
19	Oatmeal with sliced strawberries	Tuna salad with avocado	Salmon and brown rice bowl
20	Scrambled eggs with cooked carrots	Beef and potato hash	Turkey and vegetable stew
21	Greek yogurt with honey	Chicken and quinoa stir-fry	Fish and pumpkin stew
22	Boiled eggs with mashed sweet potato	Turkey and rice soup	Beef and lentil stew
23	Cottage cheese with diced pineapple	Grilled salmon with asparagus	Chicken and barley soup

24	Pumpkin and peanut butter muffins	Beef and quinoa salad	Turkey and sweet potato mash
25	Oatmeal with mashed banana	Tuna and brown rice casserole	Salmon and vegetable stir-fry
26	Scrambled eggs with cooked peas	Chicken and potato hash	Beef and rice bowl
27	Greek yogurt with diced pear	Turkey and barley stew	Fish and quinoa pilaf
28	Cottage cheese with sliced kiwi	Beef and sweet potato stir-fry	Chicken and lentil stew
29	Boiled chicken with mashed carrots	Salmon and rice salad	Turkey and quinoa pilaf
30	Peanut butter and apple slices	Tuna and vegetable stir-fry	Beef and pumpkin stew